ASBESTOS PHOENIX

ASBESTOS PHOENIX

RAMON GUTHRIE

Funk & Wagnalls   New York

ACKNOWLEDGMENTS

With two exceptions, "Postlude: for Goya," which appeared in a slightly different version in *Graffiti* (1959), and my translation of Aragon's "La Rose et le Réséda," the poems included in this volume were composed between 1960 and 1968 and comprise about a third of the poetry that I wrote during this period.

Thanks are due to the following periodicals for assignment of copyrights and permission to reprint:

The Carleton Miscellany: "Pattern for a Brocade Shroud," "On Seeing the First Woodchuck of the Spring and the Last Pterodactyl," "Springsong in East Gruesome," "Logos," "Wunday the Worst of Weptober," "Autophage."

Dartmouth Alumni Magazine: "The Back of My Mind."

Dartmouth Quarterly: "The Reseda and the Rose."

Greensleeves: "The Poet to His Mind."

Hip Pocket Poems: "A Lovely Morning at Beaumont Barracks."

The Nation: "Unveiling a Statue to a One-Time Poet."

100 Postwar Poems, British and American, M. L. Rosenthal, ed. (New York: The Macmillan Company): "Laura, Age Eight."

Poetry: "L'Enfance de la Sirène."

Quarterly Review of Literature: "Suite by the River," "They Danced," "Keepsake," "Coda."

The Quest: "Cantata for Saint Budóc's Day," "Elegy for Mélusine."

I also use this occasion to express my deepest gratitude to Alexander Laing for his encouragement, advice, and assistance during the years in which I was writing and putting together this book.

RAMON GUTHRIE

CONTENTS

V
CONVERSATION WITH THE SPHINX

VI
"FROM GOING TO AND FRO IN THE EARTH . . ."

VII
SALUTE TO SUNDRY

VIII
"IT IS MEET THAT GREEKS SHOULD RULE OVER BARBARIANS"

I

ASBESTOS
PHOENIX

"Feeling itself grow old, this bird
builds itself a pyre whereon it
mounts and is consumed. On the
ninth day thereafter it rises from
its own ashes."

—De Algunas Bestias

SUITE BY THE RIVER

I. *Brittle as Threads of Glass*

Between
talking of kingfishers and buttercups
        (if that is what they were—it seems
        the likelier name was marsh marigolds),
we fell silent
and dabbled at the river with our toes.
        Below the bridge a pickerel splashed.
                A dragonfly
perched
            with its angular four wings
and six abrupt
elbows   on the dry summit of a stone.
Three   four   five—
        look, there's another—minnows
wove upstream among the rushes.

    3, 4, 5 and 6—still another made it 7—
and four wings and six elbows
and one river
and 2 people with 1 more night together . . .
It was a very arithmetical afternoon—
    brittle as threads of glass.

II. *Alba for Mélusine*

"Et ades sera l'alba."
—GIRAUTZ DE BORNELH

Waking beside you I watch this night
dissolve inexorable into dawn.
I put words from me. No need of second sight
to scotch the lie that seas are narrow,
years short and bring no change. No,
but the hand that grips your nape
shapes its degree of meaning
and blood-beat makes this alba for our parting:

Mélusine,
may every other man ever to hold
you cool and agile in his arms
live forever—
up to the end of time and then beyond.
Death recede from him like the lake's level
from Tantalus. Coy oblivion elude him.
Aye, more: through unabridged eternity may he
grub fallow memory fruitless to conjure up
this smooth knoll of your shoulder,
this cwm of flank, this moss-delineated quite
un-Platonic cave.

May your feet's slenderness extort of him
arid invention
without reward of recollection.
May he recall you all amiss,
that mat black wilful mane of yours
as aureate floss, your eyes
(which are obsidian) as chalcedony.
Even may he grope in vain to find the feral low
tonalities of your unprecedented voice in darkness.

That easy puma prowl of yours
come back to him as a mere human gait,

4

the tanbark scent of you be in his mind
only as some vague fragrancy
of heliotrope or lilac.
                              Mélusine,
may even the name he tries to suit
his spurious evocation to
forever evade his tongue.

For that, I leave this aubade, too, unsung.

      III.   *Stalled Meteor*

Stalled somewhere along its
                              give or take
            a dozen light-years
course toward Cassiopeia
      a meteor sends forth its
S O S   MAYDAY
            but in a code
so either obsolete or so not yet invented . . .

   Meanwhile galaxies
are swishing about it
                              some
buzzing it as close as
                              say
n times the distance from here to Betelgeuse
            unknowing of its plight

            Stalled there as distant from
whatever there *is*
      to be distant from

                  as you and I
lying in the caduceus orbit of each others' arms
      impenetrably clothed in our
reciprocal nakedness

Sluiced by oncoming dawn
you are far
                    and near
shaped ivory whose gloss
lint of sleep a moment yet obscures

PATTERN FOR A BROCADE SHROUD: AFTER WATTEAU

(To L. V.)

I

Make it approximate:
          apples and antiques,
sheen muted to an autumn–crocus tint.

          The way they spoke in spirals,
     sighing, "I am sew   sew . . .
we are sew   eery . . . our fingers to the bone . . ."
          Slow centrifugal Norns
or call them Parcae
(depending on the climb or just the way
the ball bounces or the biscuit breaks)

          Curious—
as we approached the colonnade,
this golden apple of the Hesperides
came bouncing down the marble steps and splashed
into the lagoon, frightening the swans.
          . . . We never learned: for all we know
it well may be there still.

          Later
we strolled through stately glades
pausing to admire clear vistas
bordered, among the beeches and the yews,
by pipe-clayed clockwork statues in slow motion
of lean ithyphallic discoboli
dappled by sun and shade,
and masked diaphanous wood and water nymphs

playing the graces
with crystal wands and velvet hoops.

II

Cut it in swaths of river mist
    Whet the scythe in early afternoon
so that the sound comes cool
and the water squelches about our ankles
      and cowbells seem
a slightly affected anachronism in the layers
of air stacked up so high behind us.

Topaz, you said the word was,
but with the swallows skimming the pool
so close their sickle wings stirred ripples,
all I could think of was obsidian

    A distinct
    tinkle breaks the "eternal silence of
    those in*fi*nite spaces."

III

Four should be enough. If anybody asks
what we need buttons on a shroud at *all* for,
tell him it shall be answered him in time.
Let them be alternate of walrus tusk and ivory
recalling sea and sun
      awry horizons. And let the pockets be
deep and plentiful
if only to confound the adage.

IV

Two round-trip tickets to Cythera.
There was a flinty sharpness to the wine
that was not too disagreeable: it went well
with the fake–oak paneling, electric candlesticks,
and the pigeon–eyed waitress disapproving of
our knees touching beneath the table.
                                        Later,
looking up through crackled night,
we clearly heard adjacent stars
converse in muffled batsqueaks.

There was a tang of trampled leaves, a mirror
that showed us looking quite unlike ourselves
and, on the wall, a schedule of excursion trips
across the lake and a poster announcing a raffle:
            1st prize, an asbestos phoenix
            2nd prize, an adjustable Procrustean bed
            3rd prize, an imported doll made in
                    Neuchâtel (Schweiz) who, when you squeezed her,
spat in your eye and enunciated, "Fuck *you,* sir!"
There were a number of other prizes:
loves, fames, fortunes—more or less helter–skelter,
as I remember—dreamless sleeps and sleepless dreams
and, for the man who thinks he has everything,
burnished steel whippets and flights
                    of wrought copper birds.
The winning and the losing tickets cost the same.

            V

        . . . the cost the same . . . the same . . .
the winning and the losing cost the same
                            OMOI . . .
Aï de mi . . . The brain balks but the throat is riven.

9

All most a very nigh
tie weigh cup scree ming, "Home!
　　O Operator, F-U-R-I 1–2
　　　go home."
"Go where?"
　　　"Please if You don't mind, home."
Comes the automated, "For that you will have to consult
your local travel agent
or the yellow pages under real estate."
　　　(Well, as the Swiss doll said . . .)

*Spoken as distinct
syllables, dully,
with no sense of
their meaning.*

　　　There was a fragrance of moss
　　　　　　　　　　　. . . grants of moss
　　　lichen pungency of dawn
　　　　　　　　　　　. . . awn
　　　herons standing in the fallow sedges
　　　　　　　　　　　. . . shallow edges
　　　of the lake.

Come October, great honking vees of geese
on their way south will settle here to feed.
　　　Winging beneath a lid of overcast,
　　　　upward of fifty of them, so low that I could feel
　　　calls shaping in their throats, necks reaching,
　　　the pull of wing muscles. Just above
　　　the pasture crest, they went into
　　　a sudden veer, smooth, precise as if
　　　steered by a helm.
　　　　　　　　　　　I stood there long
　　　among the junipers and boulders,
　　　feeling the quiet and the chill set in.

So many speak of death who never died.
So many speak of love who know only
as much of it as lies between
thighs or books' pages.
(I speak as an old man doubting whether
he ever lived or spoke at all.)

"Le silence éternal de ces espaces infinis m'effraie."
Silence? M'effraie? No, I am making
no insinuations, proffering no exegesis—
merely wondering. After all, said by this
propounder of the Wager, this not unanguished founder
of the mathematical theory of probability . . .

Kids don't holler down the rain barrel any more.
It used to be a seasonable play
like spinning tops and making willow whistles.
Now, partly because there *are* no rain barrels
    (in part because it seldom ever rains),
kids have stopped doing it. I gave it up
one day when suddenly the thought
hit me, "What if this time no echo came?"
That it could never happen was reason more
for not daring to risk it.

      "My grandad always said to find live water
      it had to be witch hazel, although I've known
      some dowsers to use willow or even apple . . .

      "You know, I never really did enjoy
      church-going until I got around to being an atheist
      and old enough to dare to say so . . . Wasted years
      thinking I *had* to or leastwise *ought* to go . . ."

That was Uncle—great-grand-uncle—Simeon speaking.
He died at 96. The grandad he spoke of
could well have been alive when Watteau
was painting the *Embarcation for Cythera*.
In his last days he said, "Here I am in my dotage,
having to be spoon-fed, weaker than a babe
in body and brain, can't even pee
under my own power. I figure that if the Lord
wanted me to believe, he's big enough
to *make* me."

Not that he had ever played the fiddle much
nor well—a largo rendering of Turkey-in-the-Straw
about his limit—but that it had been *his*
ever since he swapped a dozen skunk skins for it
back in Andrew Jackson's first administration,
it was his wish to have it buried with him.
Of course he didn't get it. It would have seemed
a heathen sort of thing to do. Besides,
he'd have enough already to explain
without appearing at the Judgment Seat
with a warped fiddle he had never learned to play
tucked under his chin.

VII

Ho! Make it of—*Agitato ma non troppo*
                              . . . *non troppo*—
make it of best Jacquard brocade and chased
silver clips and clasps, the wings.
Spangle it with aglets and fourragères.
Ho! Deck it out with gold-fringed epaulets
and hashmarks from cuff to elbow.
Ho! Affix the medals, decorations, campaign ribbons,
        all three rows of them,
including Mexico (the deepest into which I got
was rigging up artillery targets in Tobyhanna, Pennsylvania)
and Salonika (the dispossessed storks
flapping above the crumpled minarets of Monastir;
the tall, black-purple, gut-shot Senegalese
glistening and grinning white with pain;
the donkey, forelegs planted wide apart,
braying back at the Austrian mountain battery).
Ho once more! the candystripe ribbon for being a volunteer
and the bronzy one with the tricolor piping—
        all of them, not excepting even
the Palmes Académiques with the rosette,
usually reserved for cuckolded

provincial music teachers.
Ho! sow the whole liberally with oak- and palm-leaf
                    clusters
and, Ho! when it is finished,
present it to
          The Ishmak County Historical Museum
                    —to clothe belike a taxidermic moose.

          Naked
I want to lie   naked to the
naked earth,
                    on my left side
facing the point on the horizon's rim
the sun first notches at the vernal equinox.

Will I get that? Damn right I won't!
Whole sheaves of laws, rules, statutes, ordinances
stand counter to such senile whims.

Well, what about a dolmen? I'd settle for
a dolmen. No, not a phony nor even
a dismantled, reassembled one. A small
one-owner dolmen second-hand would do.
What I have in mind is something in the line
of the one I stumbled on that summer afternoon
hidden among the yellow-blossomed broom
on the downs above a loop of the Vézère.

          VIII

Nothing to take a man up there except
an outside chance of happening upon
a tool perhaps some forbear chipped in flint
twenty milleniums ago—or utmost luck—
a bison or a reindeer he had scratched
into a patch of overhanging ledge.

(Once in an *abri* I had found a clay
loom weight astray among Solutrian celts.)

The barefoot dam in tarnished bombazeen
tending her geese beneath a fanwork vault
of chestnut trees ablaze with pollen clusters,
had warned me of the vipers. Even the poachers,
for all their leather leggings, would shun the heights
until frost came. I had shrugged her mumbling off.
But there on what could only be a dolmen's
roof or capstone, a mottled velvet coil,
slim as a willow twig, absurdly small
and frail to strike such instant awe,
raised its trim wedge-shaped head on arching neck.
Slit topaz pupils, darting tongue fixed me.

Though for the most I render gods their spite,
whatever taught that puny fellow-thing
its poise of deadly arrogance, be praised;
whatever let me never think to raise
the stick I might have killed it with, be blessed—
mean that what it may. I backed away
and watched the ribbon brightness glide between
gnarled root and riser stone.

> *Afar a fox bark echoes . . .*
>> *Hawk's shadow hovers a moment on the lichened*
>> *scree . . .*

IX

Chorus of the Parcae (They are crying raffle tickets.
Their mist-toned chitons, voluminous and transparent,
billow in a pulsing rhythm. They speak in an implosive
whisper, subdued but, once one has heard it, compelling):
> "The winning and the losing . . .
>> The winning and the losing . . .

Step up and get your tickets . . . tickets . . .
The winning and the losing cost the same . . ."

. . . Steel whippets
straining at their burnished fixity . . .
birds, the hammered copper birds,
congealed in flight . . .
Obsidian blade, clattering to the altar stone,
breaks with a ping like crystal . . .

Portent of autumn, a scattered burst
of raindrops sweeps
an oak-stained pool of the Vézère.

NOTES FOR "PATTERN FOR A BROCADE SHROUD"

PART I

Watteau: The reference is to his *Embarquement pour Cythère, Jugement de Paris,* and the *fêtes galantes.*
Autumn crocus: A stemless perennial with pale-lavender flowers. It grows wild in meadows in parts of Europe.
Norns: In Teutonic myth, these demigoddesses, corresponding to the Parcae, weave the weirds of both men and gods.
The graces: A game in which the players, each using two wands, toss a small hoop, often covered with velvet, back and forth.

PART VII

Tobyhanna: An army post where National Guard artillery units mustered into federal service at the time of the American punitive expedition into Mexico were trained.

Monastir: A city in Macedonia. In 1917 the French forces, consisting largely of colonial troops, tried to break through the Germans, Austrians, and Bulgars positioned in a semicircle of mountains above the town.

Palmes académiques: Every few years the French government insists on awarding me this decoration, with or without rosette. I can't imagine why.

Dolmen: These megalithic burial chambers (*circa* 2300–1000 B.C.) usually consist of a capstone supported by a number of side slabs planted vertically in the earth. They are found throughout most of France. In a cemetery at Meudon, in the suburbs of Paris, is a dolmen that was dismantled and transported from Brittany to serve as a family tomb.

Vézère: Before cocacolonization came along, the Vézère was one of the loveliest of rivers. Of late years, many of its fine medieval bridges have been replaced by cement and iron ones.

II

RIGADOONS AND DOXOLOGIES

LOGOS

Untethered from words
Poetry could be the most—
        or better say, the only—
autonomous impulse in the world

    But then of course
there would *be* no world
        which, when you come to think of it,
might not be too great a loss.

    Imagine waking up one bright
Monday morning and—WHEE!
    Look, mom, no world!
and it isn't even monday either
        for that matter . . .

            nothing Except
one taut tenseless
        transitive Verb
        immune alike to subject and object
whose function poetry is
        to parse
throughout a pristine millenium—

        a Judgment Day
in which the whole expanding universe
is the great big bouncing Booby Prize

till good old
(or bad old, depending on how you look at it)
Gitchi Manitou
touches it with the business end of His cigar

PWOP!

Shucks, don't you blubber, son. They's plenty more
where that came from.
Here, take a pocketful and blow 'em up yourself.

UNVEILING A STATUE
TO A ONE-TIME POET

(According to Lactantius, neither Apollo's flute, Hermes' lyre, nor the song of the dying swan can compare with the Phoenix's song.)

In plaster effigy here stands the gawking
hero who grabbed the Phoenix with bare hands
    (Skoal, slante, to his glory growing dim!)

Clutched by its shanks, flapping, squawking,
it battered him with wings. Its beak
jabbed out his eyes. Anus bespattered him
with noisome mutings. To the surprise
of all our clique, he held it for an instant—thus!—
quite as unmarvelous in its disarray
as bald-necked turkey or a moulting owl—
before it broke his grip and soared away.

      Through years, aging,
sightless, savaged, numb—unmanned, said some—
by the ignominious, emerald-shimmering fowl,
we used to see him groping down the street,
slavering in bistros, cadging beers,
boasting in varying versions of his feat—
claimed he had caged it, learned of it to sing
in modes too sublimate for mortal ears.
On one puke-sodden bender he even told
of roasting it: the breast, he said, was tender,
the drumstick acrid, tough,
the gizzard flecked with gold.

There came a night when we had had enough
and heaved him out. He landed on his head,
the night was cold, at closing time we found him dead.

So less in admiration than relief
and with no more remorse than is expected
of Moira's agents, no pretense of grief,
we passed the hat and had this form erected.

Dismissing bronze or marble, we chose plaster
as easier to work, less costly, crumbling faster.
For interest—since the fellow had no face
except the havoc that the Phoenix wrought,
lingam and yoni ornament the base:
they bulked so largely in his latter thought.

L'ENFANCE DE LA SIRÈNE

(The juice of the wilted leaves
of black nightshade is a lethal
narcotic. Argos was Odysseus'
dog, who died of joy on recog-
nizing his master after twenty
years absence.)

New canticle in mode of moss and amber—
sea wrack—
   (*bramble twitched by the sirocco*
   etched the diagram on sand)
scrived at last from the sheer headland,
emerges as first girl. Naked surprise
incised in every poise
to see her footprints patterned on the beach,
she threads through throngs of phantom lovers.
They reach to her. Not one of them perceives
she casts no shadow.
Assuming substance, they straggle back to cities
by devious routes. Later they will slake
bewilderments on trampled grass
bestrewn with cigarette butts and condoms
or on crumpled beds,
with botched facsimiles, hips creased with weals
               of garter belts,

For no clear mountain pool
               spilling over white pebbles,
they will wade pelvis-deep amid
water-striders and frog spawn.

The wise among them
will ask themselves no questions.
They will plug their ears with wax, lean to the oars
—yet to no homecomings.
                              The fools among them
will find native lands everywhere,
expatriate themselves from all of them.

Wherever the girl that is a canticle has passed,
they will turn up there late or soon.
Once their feet have touched the nightshade fringes
of her shadow, they will forever return
to where they have never been.

Their homecomings will be at furtive
street corners in the rain, their Penelopes
callgirls with forgotten telephone numbers.

Argos will bite them. They will be on their ways.

HOMAGE TO PAUL DELVAUX
(1897-   )

Everywhere about is landscape as far as foot can feel
lamps exude their light on flagstones
there are quaint quiet trains in
corridors of pure perspective

Out of this span of calm I rise
to hear irises unfold   moss grow infallibly
on north bark of larches   Death in temporary form
of Paul Delvaux's discreetly pubic girls
bedmates of gone goddesses walking in gardens of
undeflowered music and undeciphered roses
while waiting for their mutual dream to bring about
eclipses of the moon

I walk a long while and wait
I wait a long while and walk
I peer into a well and see a fountain
I peer into a fountain and see
the crystal chrysalis of a chaste nymph
rising toward the sliver of a moon

We load our last possessions on a raft
and hoist the makeshift sail
Our awkward innocence defies return
We know this
We feel a deep alarm but do not speak

                    Ten deliberate
adjectives too many for one volcanic

somnambulistic mound dormant but
aquiver
       fox in April in the sun

             frisson ou pas frisson
                frisson   frisson   pas frisson
          frisson en avril

IT HAPPENS

(To M.C.)

It happens
        has no name
No word stands in its path   delimits it
It happens when Goya paints
       those gloves   that pock-marked wondrous face
of the Marquesa de la Solana
When Uccello makes
       those sniggering barrel-bellied steeds
(Horse thou never wert!) and reed-like
       stands of lances
             When Gislebertus
chisels out his Eve and Simon Magus
circa 1130 at Autun   Yes
and it happens in Stendhal's sly
     ". . . offrait à Julien   du vin du Rhin
     dans un verre vert"

In quite a different mode and vocabulary
it is what the lone
detached
       steeple at Vendôme is speaking clear
of a summer evening or a winter morning
     when there is fog and snow
It is as brightly unelaborate as Sisley's
morning of the flood at Port-Marly
or Villon's "Laissons le moustier où il est"
     or again as
chromatically positive and flat
as Picasso's brothel in Avignon

It has little to do
with graces and sonorities
and is essentially incorrect
by any standards but its own

Such congruities as it has
are incidental counterpoint
of hailstones on
slate   in zinc gutters   on lawns

It happens as
still eruption spurt
    of seed

In instants when delight and anguish
cancel each other out in shrill conjunction
    it happens

Girl standing by herself atop
a stubbled hillock
tugged at   tousled by
November wind

Disembodied fury
crumbling geodes in its bare fists
A one-armed red   by name José Clemente
working with an absurdly small
watercolor brush on wet plaster gives us his fierce serene
    Descent from the Cross
Braced   axe-wielding Christ more living
for every death He dies for us
More glorious for every degradation

        At Auvers
the red gash of road that straggled
across the wheatfield to the cemetery

has been leveled and black-topped
    the verdigris clouds and
39 crows effaced   Their flight remains

            It happens
Moan on a sweltering Brooklyn night
            (fire-escape complete with painted
                    velvet cushion and transistor
"Oh, lover, hurt me hard!")
                    Rigor vitae setting in

Yes   it can happen that way too

It happens of its own
                sharp need to its own immediacy

It happens in shouts or whispers or silence
        in chords and crescendi
                    not yet set on scores
in the tread of many thousand feet
        walking in the rain

        Do not name it
It is holy   has no name

        It happens

    Not seen her
scarcely heard her name
in these near twenty years
                    I doddering when she
        was earning Girl Scout badges and
                pigtails flying
        winning ribbons in slaloms over boys
Now she (Sister Saint Johannus in religion) learning I
(still staunch Stendhalian)

am once more scalpels' game   writes
   and says "love" 3 times on the sides
            of a single page
and "always kept you in my special prayers"

                              And means it
                              And it means

It is holy   has no name
It happens
                    Do not name it

It happens in faces
      bloodied bruised by rifle butts

It happens

            The fragile
quaintly neat spinster
      crouched in the screech of traffic
            bleat of klaxons
cradles the ancient mongrel's grey
muzzle to her flat chest and speaks
tenderness   reassurance to his
      long deaf   now dead
ears
            half imagines
she sees his tail wag recognition
                              Pietà

   It happens
         Oh   I too
      could sometimes shout or sing or sob
         wild hosannas to Its name

EXEGESIS

No, lady, the foregoing poem is neither
a riddle nor a rebus. Nothing to be guessed.
When it says, "It has no name," it means just that.
No, not "grace," "vision," "caritas,"
or some exuberant, all-embracing, new,
exhilarating virtue that God and I
have just concocted.

Look, read the thing again, taking it literally.
You are handicapped by thinking of me as having
some eldritch pact with words. Whereas—
groping drop-out from night-school,
lifelong at odds with them for their chicanery and despotism—
I consort with words only from sheer loneliness,
as a lifer in solitary might welcome
the companionship of a spider or a cockroach.

                    Listen . . .
No, that is asking too much. Even as I set to speak,
you gasp, "How fascinating it must be to live
in that mind of yours where everything
is glistening new and subtle and alive!
I often wonder what it must be like."

Hold tight! I am about to tell you. Mostly
it is like being a nightwatchman in a morgue
where it is always night and all of the cadavers
suffer from perpetual insomnia
even in their most excruciating nightmares,
while he himself lives in continual sick dread
of being fired.

THEY DANCED

Off and on they danced

They danced round and round
        and up and down
They danced back and forth
        and sidewise

They danced on tiptoes and tombstones
They danced on empty stomachs and tin roofs
They danced on purpose and on a moment's notice
                on dolmens and menhirs
They danced on Saint Budóc's day
        and on Saint Cornély's
        and on the Eves of Saint Winok'h
        and Saint Melio, Cornish King,
On and on and on they danced

They danced to
                musettes and rebecs
They danced to large and small audiences
They danced to while away the time
They danced to and fro
They danced to jews-harps and kazoos
They danced to Jericho and back
They danced to end all dancing
They danced to rigadoons and doxologies

They danced in
They danced in couples and quadrilles

They danced in clearings and guildhalls
They danced in unison and in secret
They danced in measure
                in brains and veins
They danced in vain alas
They danced in trances and in protest
They danced in G-strings and singlets
                In spite of everything
they danced.

They danced on and on and on
and in the end
        they danced off

strewing behind them sequels
of sequins and concetti
residues of one-owner skills and skulls
and bastard urchins to boot

NOTES FOR "THEY DANCED"

Saint Budóc: Most of the popular Breton saints are not to be found
in orthodox hagiographies. Saint Budóc immigrated from Ireland
to Brittany on a floating stone. Saint Cornély, patron of horned
animals, fled from Rome with his two pet oxen. When the Roman
soldiers who were pursuing him cornered him against the sea near
Carnac, he turned them into the great alignments of granite
menhirs that still stand there. Saint Winok'h was wont to go on
such homicidal drunks that he had to be kept chained up in his
cell. As for Saint Melio, he was a King who was murdered by his

brother in 538 A.D.; the splendid parish close of Guimiliau commemorates him.

Urchins: The reference is mainly to sea-urchins (*oursins*) and obliquely to an elderly Mr.-Chips-like Englishman who used to startle new acquaintances by innocently confessing that the reason he chose to live in Marseilles was that he "so adored the urchins," meaning the echinoderms, locally esteemed as a delicacy, that are sold and eaten generally *sur place,* along the quai of the Vieux Port. He lived with a stocky girl named Gasparde, who looked like an unbathed bison. She chose his ties, shined his shoes and, all Anglican that he was, took him to Mass every Sunday.

CANTATA FOR
SAINT BUDÓC'S DAY

*Nam et vere dictum est quod
sanctus Budocus a Scotia in
Armoricam in lapide navigavit.*
—DE SANCTIS CORNUBII.

Says what? Whole swags and gaggles of 'em?
Mud-hawks and pismires half a spindle long?
And ye've a feared of 'em? What be ye—many mice?
Spankers a-hoo! And did not Saint Budóc
sail a stone a-float from Ballyhack to Brittany—
dead reckoning no less, with neither binnacle nor helm?
Barong! I'll show ye how to set to proper up a bilge.
Lobster-long scorpiums, you say?
beetle-bugs that squirt snuff at ye?
swift-skittering spiders the size of griddlecakes?
A-back! Broom-room is all I ask,
and in a whisk . . .
$\qquad\qquad\qquad$ Hee-yipes! and here they come!
—Didn't ye'd ought of warned a man!—
swarming up broom handle and inside
sleeves and pants legs, cruftier than sprikes!
$\qquad$ Har-*rook!* Har-rook! and if aught a one
aver I'm not scairt flealess,
I'll daunt him to defend it. Har*rook!*
Stand clear! I'm out of here. Ye canna keep
a good man down—*and that's an adage!*
You with the leather beard!
You with the mink ear-muffs!
Take on where I left off. I'm needed elsewhere.
Urgenter deeds attend me.

Har*rook*, old hamster, you honk-nosed janissary!
Hindle me not, ye horehounds, lest ye'd be holystoned.
Harrook! Can't ye not see I'm hasping down the halyards?
Harrook, ye meddlestrums. Unhook your harps from here!
     Harrook!
Screech ears for Saint Budóc whose day it is.
    Hark!   Hark!   Harrook!

A LOVELY MORNING AT
BEAUMONT BARRACKS

The drummer beat tattoo
and everybody said,
"What is he doing that for?
What the hell is he doing that for?
This is a lovely morning."

The bugler sounded mess call
followed immediately by taps—
taps in the daytime—
and everyone looked puzzled
and milled about this way and that.
"What did he do that for?
Who is being buried
and who is eating what—
on such a lovely morning?"

The girls came trickling out from town
to see the parade
and found it was a funeral instead
with full military honors.
"Stick around. Stick around, Elizabeth.
Stick around, Karen and Clorinda, Mary Ann,
Ginette and Yetta and Yolanda.
Fall in with us and come along.
As soon as we get this mess unscrambled,
as soon as we get this buzzard in the ground,
we're having a champagne breakfast.
                    And anyway
this *is* a lovely morning."

The girls fell in ranks with the soldiers
marching arm-in-arm
over the hill to the cemetery
with rifles reversed and muffled drums
and the band playing a medley
of *Happy Days Are Here Again*
and the Dead March from *Saul*.
When they got there it was discovered
that someone had forgotten to provide a corpse
(that would be fixed up later, drawing lots).
The chaplain read the service anyway,
and it *still* was a lovely morning.
      The girls were lovely too
      swinging along with their gayly-striped tote-bags
      arm-in-arm with the soldiers.

It was so lovely a morning
that the firing-squad was not detailed
until after the champagne brunch.
Then the prettiest girl picked a name from a hat.
"Sergeant McRary, you win! You've won!"

They stood him up blank against the wall
and teasingly called him Danny Deever
and made believe feel his brow for fever.
His girl, who was a gypsy,
had come on purpose from Poughkeepsie.
Triggers clicked. The Lieut said, "Damn-oh!
They forgot to issue ammo!"
So they didn't shoot him that day or at all.

Surprised at finding himself not dead,
the Sergeant yawned and stretched and said,
"It *was* a *lovely* morning!"

They had no reason, no reason at all,
for having wasted a fu-ne-ral
but it *was* a lov-e-ly morning.

LAURA AGE EIGHT

(She falls asleep across the
arm of a sofa)

When this young *objet trouvé* improvises sleep
she formulates new definitions
        of grace and even comfort
as absurd
                and vice versa
as they are authentic

        Eyelashes against contour of a
cheek and nose tip
                coiled limber spine
sprawled disrupted skein of
        elbows   knees   shins
                                sneakered feet
mane whose pendant weight would be
        wasted on a pillow

This abrupt repose is of no single kingdom
                Cats and catkins have it
        colts and ferns and wild
columbine

        And in the mineral realm
some of the more improbably
        spontaneous crystals

        Patterns akin to this sometimes turn up
on beaches
                as intricately twined
roots of driftwood.

III

MARSYAS
IN THE INTENSIVE
CARE WARD

I. *Red-headed Interne, Taking Notes*

Do you been or did you never? Ha!
Speakless, can you flex your omohyoid
and whinny ninety-nine? Quick now,
can you recall your grandmother's maiden name
six times rapidly? Have you a phobia of spiders?
Only fairly large and brown ones
dropping from the ceiling?
Does this happen often, would you say?
(Nurse, clamp the necrometer when I say when.
If he passes out, tickle his nose with a burning feather
and tweak his ears counterclockwise.)
        No history of zombi-ism in the immediate family?
And tularemia? No recent intercourse
with a rabbit?
        (Lash him firmly to the stretcher
        and store him in the ghast house for the night.)

II. *Via Crucis*

Out of this   coming sidewise   slinking and
        sidling two steps forward and nine or ten
backward for fear of getting a charge of rock-salt
for a Peeping Tom . . . Gangway, lady! Gangway!
I'm doing a via crucis.
And she says, "B'jazes, it's the first time I ever seen
anybody doing a Way of the Cross
in a hospital johnny! What are you—
a furriner or something?"
        Thou sayest it, lady. All these years
I've been wondering what I am and now I know:
        a foreigner or something. No kith, belike,
or kin of anything—at least among the higher primates—
a biologically speaking, sport!

43

By what, for all its blare, must still be night,
the swift square-bottomed nurse flits sure
from bed to bed, takes blood pressures and pulses,
checks drains and bandages, switches on chest pumps.
Internes, doctors, moving in pairs,
converse in muffled nods. Approaching with a clip-board,
a small wren-faced nurse asks, "Sir,
what is your religion?" Religion?
"I have to ask you just in case." None.
She marks the X at Protestant.

MR. GOLDBLATT: STAFF NURSE (white letters on
blue plastic badge) buzzing like an officious
bottlefly doing an imitation of Schnozzle Durante,
struts in by what, if they would give me back my watch,
must now be morning. There are no windows though
to judge that by, only these cones of light
trained on our eyelids . . . high iron grills
fencing in each of the nearly touching beds
constantly being (one man dying or making guggling
sounds of death, another in new-bloodied bandages
arriving) trundled in or out.

   "HELLO, OL' SPORT! How you doin', ol' sport?
Come on, ol' sport, roll over so I can insert . . .
Look here, ol' sport, you just always do
just like I tell you and we'll get along fine."

Maximum Security Ward. Sure, I know . . .
Intensive Care Ward, but none the less,
straight out of Jacques Callot by Hogarth.
   "What time they bring him in here? 2 a.m.?"

No, so to speak, white corpuscles. Your guess
why not, as good as mine: all I know

is chattering teeth and thirst.
   "Look here, ol' sport.
I give you ginger ale a while ago.
You'da been thirsty, you'da drunk it
instead of yammerin' for water now.
You don't like ginger ale, it ain't my fault.
I'm busy now, I got my records to keep up."

MR. GOLDBLATT, you cloacal-breathed, glad-handing ghoul,
if ever I get my white
corpuscules out of hock
and temperature down enough to take it orally,
I'm going to vault that bedrail and ram
those outsized, clicking dentures down your throat,
God be my witness. SELAH.

III.   *Elegy for Mélusine from the*
Intensive Care Ward

So name her Vivian. I, scarecrow Merlin,
our Broceliande this frantic bramble of
glass and rubber tubes and stainless steel,
could count off such illusions as I have
on a quarter of my thumbs.

     (. . . *even a postcard of Viollet-le-Duc's*
pensive chimera signed with her initial . . .)

I penciled out a cable: FCHRISAKE COMMA
WRITE TO ME STOP YOURE LIVING AND IM DYING.
Nurse challenged the expletive and my assurance
that it was an Ainu epithet of endearment.
I struck out everything but WRITE—cheaper

and beside I wasn't really dying
save that I couldn't breathe too well
nor feed except on intravenous dextrose.

Still stands that I am dying, Mélusine,
and have been ever since my infancy,
but the process is more measurable now.
You can tick off the months on a calendar—
eeny, meeny, miny . . . and when you get to the end . . .

> *(Today again no word.*
> *. . . Breton Saint Anne . . . Black Virgin*
> *of Le Puy . . .)*

When you get to the end . . .
when you get to the end . . .
You know what *I* should like to do when I get to the end?
when I am tucked and snug and smug
with hair combed sleek for once
pants pressed   shoes shined
and tie on straight for the first time in my life?

I'd like to give one last galvanic jerk
and flip up straight and look all living beings
in the eye—all human ones, that is
(because, less lucky than are cats and cows
and bumblebees, they know that they are living)
and speak out clear: "I hate life. I who am
no longer living can speak this truth.
From my first taste of it, from the moment when
my drunken Uncle Doc dangled me by the heels
and whacked my rump, I have always hated living!"
then flop back flat into the casket with a happy
or, at least, contented or vacuous, smirk upon my face—
soundly dead for keeps this time.
That, mes amis, would be worth living long enough to see!

Every tear would dry like sizzled spit
testing a hot flatiron. The organ,
up to then simpering stately lullabies,
would burst a dozen pipes. The pall-bearers
would stop dead in their tracks. (Their tracks to *where*?
Don't ask *me*: I'm only playing the lead
in this production, not directing it.)
And everybody from the preacher down
to the boy soprano, would look each other in the eye
and murmur in unison:
"Why, the old bastard! Who'da thunk it of him!"
(It would be no time for grammatical niceties.)

Still . . .
bring on your Dead March with Muffled Drums
and Reversed Rifles and high-stepping young
Drum Majorettes with the minniest of Miniskirts.
Let Taps be played and Keeners keen.
Consume the Baked Meats with good appetite.
And . . .
grant me this: I *tried* to love life—
tried my damnedest but just couldn't make it.
Matter of acquired tastes perhaps—
acquired tastes you somehow can't acquire—
like some wines (Tokay, Monbazillac)
or foods (gazpacho, prune whip, lemon pie).

Fell fable of the fox that did at last
leap high enough and the grapes
definitely *were* sour.

(. . . *or an empty envelope addressed in her concise
swift runic hand.*)

IV. *Scene: A Bedside in the Witches' Kitchen*

DOCTOR *to his retinue of internes:*
>Obvious ptoritus of the drabia.
>Although the prizzle presents no sign of rabies,
>note this pang in the upper diaphrosis.
>When kicked there hard enough, the patient utters,
>"Yoof!" and curls up like a cutworm.
>I prescribe bedcheck every hour on the hour
>with intensive catalepsis. (*Exeunt.*)

PATIENT *to Nurse:*
>My name is Marsyas, a stranger here.
>   How to explain?
>Sprächen zoo something? anything? Aard-vark? Gnu?
>You look well-meaning. If I made noises in my phlarynx
>and shaped them with my phtongue, would they have
>snignifigance to you? Or would they merely
>confuse us further? Let's go about it anagogically.
>Close your ears. Go twine your sphygnomanometer
>about some other patient or administer him his hemlock,
>while I supplicate.

>   Today is Friday.

>Gamut of goddesses, Gaia, Latona, Frigg whose day it is,
>cat-flanked Ishtar with the up-turned palms,
>Rosmertha of the Gauls, with grief-gouged eyes
>and rough-hewn cleft—
>   sister, mother, mistress of the dead,
>mare-shaped Epona, you, Venus of Lespugue
>in mammoth tusk, majestic at scarce a handsbreadth tall,
>though not quite small enough to put into a matchbox
>and walk the streets of Montparnasse with in your pocket . . .

>Gamut of goddesses,
>in your spare moments intercede for me . . .
>   (Breath comes scant now,

48

                    but by chance you may have heard,
                         my name is Marsyas) . . .
            intercede for me. Let me be never born.
            Let my ghost wander in brambled upland meadows.
            Drizzle in evening streets, may she at times recall
            our walking there, arms pressed to ribs together.

IV

HALF-PAST
HALLOWE'EN

THE BACK OF MY MIND

"I'm not sure what he has in
the back of his mind."
—ALEXANDER LAING

I

In the back of my mind,
wearing a Keystone cop's
helmet cocked over one ear and a
jovial smirk on his face, a tame hyena
who owes his post to being the only
mammal that comes by laughter honestly
patrols a maze of cobbled alleys
between high-gabled fronts with leaded panes.

He taps the creaking tavern signs
with his nightstick (it *being*
night) and cadges handouts
at surreptitiously opened
doors along his beat.

In the back of my mind
a conscientious ape crinkles his forehead
over the latest lesson of
his correspondance course
in non-Euclidean geometry.

In the back of my mind
a perennial cricket chirps a sardana
that a strait, tight-lipped
marquesa out of Goya dances

                    slowly
                              slowly
                                        slowly
and then with sudden vivacity
in the back of my mind.

                    II

On the floor of the back of my mind
lies a single petal of a silver rose
by Stéphane Mallarmé
On the wall is a fly-specked timetable
of trains that long since left
for undisclosed destinations
In the back of my mind
are a broken ivory prayer wheel
acquired by some tea-trade ancestor . . . and a
stuffed parrot that squawks,
          "Oom mani padme hum."

In the back of my mind
is the refrain of Bertran's lost song:
          "Ai, Lemozi, francha terra cortesa!"
And a slim-hipped Babylonian
alabaster doll or idol (Ishtar?)
with garnet eyes and gilded crescent in her hair
evinces no surprise
at the latest strides of science
in producing both
positive and negative non-realities.

                    III

In the back of my mind
are a tired green eyeshade and
chewed blue pencils and,

spiked on the copy file, a faded
note: "Gone to the Dutchman's for a quick one."

In the cellar is a sundial
It is always
half-past hallowe'en
in the back of my mind.

CODA

"On pourrait dire de son oeuvre qu'elle est un auto-portrait constamment retouché."
—L. Véza: Etudes
Anglaises, t. xx, No. 1.

I

Actually
neither quite Ghibelline nor Guelph.
Quince-nourished—
sated, crammed with them in such years
as quince trees flourished
till the pantry shelf was jammed with them,
I grew toward
manhood. Educated? Privately tutored—
by myself (this much is factually
true.)

II

Since,
cherubim have chirped at me,
cheery as fireworks in parks,
and frumpish Furies smirked at me. Cast
into tumbled seas and dodging sharks,
safe in the skin of a great fish
I came to Nineveh. I have been chaste
through groves where the last
lascive dryads lurked.

So say "a constantly retouched
self-portrait" to be hung upon the wall
of some quaint village bordel tucked
in a lane between the church's apse
and the charnel house perhaps—
retreat where local poet, and drunk,
and prentice little strumpet all
may stoke the stove and think
of how the lives they clutched
will close in town clerk's pale
ink, brewed from oak
gall.

III

Or better, since we all are caught in
the same impervious caul,
let's quench all thought in
a witless game we'll improvise.
Let's say a queen and jack make 69
And aces and a king count 24.
From there, you make up *your* rules, I'll make mine.
And Gretchen here can try to keep the score . . .
But, look! The Queen of Spades! She lies
face-up on the floor!

IV

Rusty as owls, the church clock jangles one.
There'll be no clients now. We stack the chips.
A deeper night's begun. The Dog Star howls.
The drunk squints at his flask for some last sips.
He starts to spy ants now—huge ants galore,
whetting their antennae for the kill.
Gretchen yawns relief and locks the till.
This is the hour of the apocalypse.

She stands like Eden's angel at the door.
Drunk brandishes his flask at the ant droves.
Before she shoves us out into the night,
Gretchen, firm but doggedly polite,
stops to ask,
"What do poets do beside just write?"

V

Now I lay me down in bed,
a nightjar clucks a lullaby.
Freud himself concocts my dream
wherein, distraught and shy,
Cassandra proffers me her maidenhead,
among the rushes by Scamander's stream.
But if I die before I wake,
The Lord mayn't find too much to take.

What *does* the poet when the vein runs out?
He sweats cold sweat and squirms to doubt his doubt.
Scanning the skies and cursing them once more,
village Prometheus, he looks to viticulture
to conjure up a liver-loving vulture—
and stares at the spade queen there on the floor.

ON SEEING THE FIRST WOODCHUCK
OF THE SPRING
AND THE LAST PTERODACTYL

Woodchuck, if you should ask me
how one makes a poem
(stranger things than that *have* happened)
I should say
Lord, chuck, I don't know,
much the way a woodchuck
makes a burrow I imagine

You pick a likely terrain
and start digging
Follow the underground pattern in the dark
Your paws know where they are going
Don't ask them
Follow them

Make it deep enough to thwart
a poem's natural enemies
and devious enough to baffle them
Make entrances enough
to have it accessible and let the air in

Live in it a while
and alter it
shape it to your needs
After all a poem is meant to be lived in
to be gone in and out of
and to learn from

If a poet should ask me how I make a poem
I should say
I've always wondered myself.

If Ilse asked me how I make a poem
I should tell her
It is a very complicated and arcane process
In simplest analogy
it is rather like making a pterodactyl pie
First you mix your piecrust
using plenty of shortening
roll it yet keep it crisp and flaky
Then you plant an acorn
When the oak is fully grown
you lime its branches
and lie in wait for it to catch
a pterodactyl.

        Listen, Ilse,
if there is any joke in this
it is on me
on me and all the eons I've sat
beneath the oak and
even hearing the tussle and the squawks
not dared look up for fear there'd be
no pterodactyl   Yes
if I asked myself
many if not all
poems are pterodactyl pies

I could not tell this to the woodchuck
I could not tell it to a poet
Each would have his own
private dicta and terminologies
The poet comes by them by osmosis
The woodchuck has four months of hibernation
to dream them up

N.B.

They must be real
pterodactyls.
Always one
is bound to be the last.

SPRINGSONG IN
EAST GRUESOME, VERMONT

(On being sent to the feedstore
to buy bonemeal, dried blood,
arsenate of lead, and other gar-
den needs.)

Little Miss Pingry answered demurely
when asked how Mamma was, "Thank you, poorly,"
in gingham and sunbonnet lowered her eyes
to her pinafored lap with its shin-sharp thighs
and did her daintiest not to drool
as she gnawed on the ulna of a ghoul
with neat little teeth so pointed and bright
that I think I shall not sleep tonight.
> (*And the wind slinks down from Mount Horrid
> to rattle the corncrib slats.*)

Miss Lettie Grigsbee's eldest pig
was named Doremus. Who *gives* a fig
for the tittletat spite that her neighbors vent
of the grunt he uttered and what it meant
when, leaning his elbows over the sty,
an itinerant butcher offered to buy
and of how she began to jerk and slaver—
as she has ever since—at the shock it gave her?
> (*And the wind scuttles over the stubble
> snatching the scarecrows' hats.*)

Deacon Bigelow, whiskers aflame
from a leaky lantern, bellowed a name
that only once in a thousand years
had ever been heard by human ears.

The weathervane squealed, the lightning-rods
writhed on the lawn, peas popped from their pods,
swallows dropped dead from the crackled sky,
and three hump-shouldered owls trudged by.
   (*And the wind is fretting the mortar
       out from the chimney bricks.*)

Old Mrs. Dreed, marshamallow fat,
kept a prim white mouse and an albino bat.
Her hope was to mate them just to see
what manner of beast their get would be.
When nothing happened, in despair
she fashioned an image and said a prayer.
She fashioned it out of gingerbread
that she pricked with a needle until it bled.
   (*And the wind went whimpering over the hill
       knowing the end of such tricks.*)

THE SWALLOWS OF CAPISTRANO

Hello! Hello? Hello, Superintendant?
Hello, Superintendant, I want to know
what all those conquistadors are doing
out there in the patio. What are they doing
out there soggily shaking termites out of their
great-boots and codpieces? And why are those
willowy widows right out of Winterhalter
ogling those cigarstore Indians so brazenly?
I find it quite upsetting. I *demand*
an explanation! And don't you dare
tell me I am *seeing* things!

No, lady, you ain't seeing much
        that I ain't seeing myself.
Only with me it's just a wooden Indian
getting barby-cued by a troop of bare-assed
Camp Fire Girls with daffydillies in their hair.

It don't upset me none. The way I see it,
it's just it's coming spring.

Now, if I was to see
blue rats crawling out of the walls
with football helmets on,
that would upset me. This stuff, no.
I just had the radio on when you called me,
hearing about them sparrers coming back to Capistrano.
Anything can happen when it's spring.

KEEPSAKE

being at three
she five
and having followed her beckon
through the crawl hole
under the latticed stoop
Gerty Brukstis being so direct about it
(purpose mud from dust)
that
even as I did not grasp it   then
so now
well past half a century
of countless confirmations
I still cannot
(save intellectually—and even then)
believe that it is
that simple   *that* smoothly
cleft and moulded
as by a deft final swipe   of some
unusually understanding god's
index or an angel's edgèd quill

that easily and *that* supremely
good
Or that anything since Attic *lékuthoi*
could be that aptly and unobtrusively
designed
Let alone
executed.

THE NEUTRINO
AND MR. BRINSLEY

"I think poetry should be so
simple that everybody can un-
derstand it—just like Nature."
—MR. BRINSLEY

We poets may snatch our inspiration from mabsolutely
manything. Majestic mice, more minuscule mountains
or even miscegenate mermaids will touch us off.

Take the neutrino—of which we know the less
the more we know about it. Nevertheless
the neutrino, in a manner of speaking, *is*—
though its manner of speaking is definitely not
that of Palgrave's *Golden Treasury.*

                                        You may
expound cosmology to a flower in a crannied wall,
try to convince a lark that it never was a bird.
As confidants of one's intimate frustrations,
field mice may prove as satisfactory as
psychiatrists, and they are easier to spell.
But, if you ever find yourself holding sweet converse
with a neutrino, better watch it!

                        That said,
no, X does not mark the spot, because
        it isn't *there* any more
        and wasn't there in the first place—
not in any accepted sense of the word *there* . . .
since, by any weekday sort of reasoning,
that which is *is,* and that which isn't,
concommitantly, is *not.* And that which, being,

66

in the phenomenal sense, discrete
yet has not mass, is (in this same
phenomenal sense) *not*.
                              Which,
since they are traveling nonstop at some
186,000 miles a second and can penetrate
a wall of anything up to ten billion
                    earth-diameters thick,
is just as well.

No, they have no electric charges and aren't
anything. Yet there are already four
known varieties of them
and probably more to come.

They are so small that the question arises
as to how and whether that which has no mass
can have relative size enough
to be smaller than something else.

It seems that near Johannesburg,
10,425 feet underground,
scientists have contrived this brobdingnagian
contraption that spatters out n billion
billions of them per second
and when, at rare intervals, *ONE*
        of them happens to hit something,
THAT, by golly,
            is known as a (quote) "event,"
            though to the uninitiate, one of them ever
managing *not* to hit something would seem to be a
        downright
                        impossibly
                                    miraculous
miracle of the first water.

Yes, Mr. Brinsley, I concede the validity
of your objection that sometimes poetry is too obscure
for the average layman readily to grasp.

What was it that the man said
about art imitating nature?

I'm not all that sure I believe it,
but there it is.

V

CONVERSATION
WITH
THE SPHINX

ORACLE FOR LEANDER

I

Oh, there is Evident Design in this
the prefab template of the tragic hero,
oracularly sure catabasis:
The square of the hypothesis is zero.

The Queen Ape turns uneasy to her drone.
With apotheosis beyond her reach,
she pats the seat beside her on the throne.
He, mixing signals, proffers her a peach

which she incontinent declines. She tries
sign language, quite forgetting he is blind.
She taps it out in Morse. It comes out lies—
or platitudes. To this they are resigned.

II

Back in the ages when a plane had struts,
he lolled, a dolphin, in the Milky Way,
molting the Leonids of bolts and nuts
he purposed to retrieve, come Judgment Day.

Or see his Astral Body skim the roofs
beneath which lovers sleep, their limbs entwined,
till, one by one, his gods sprout cloven hoofs
and thumb their files for pacts his blood has signed.

Now, swimming against a tide between no shores,
leaden Leander to a Lot's wife Hero,
he reads the verdict, Braille in madrepores:
The square of the hypothesis is O.

THE POET TO HIS MIND

        My mind
at your most attractive
at those rare moments when I would not
        gladly turn you in
on an acute
case of chronic priapism   or self-replacing teeth
        you are
                a half-grown cat   too leggy to be a kitten
        You prance arch-backed
                        and pounce on unsuspecting
ideas and concepts
        clutch them with claws
                        bite   rake them with both
        hind legs at once
toss them in the air   catch them   And
an instant short of boredom   conveniently contrive
to lose them   under the divan
or the radio or God
        (shall we say
                        since He is not
        entirely alien to these considerations)
knows where
                        Then you
lick one paw   wash the handiest
        ear and fall asleep

        Sometimes
I am not too sure that
        some of the more august among these entities
relish being cast as catnip mice.

RECITAL FOR OBOES
AND A KETTLEDRUM

that year Judgment Day
fell on tuesday
—WHOOM! (muted by earthquake claps
of bells and thunder)
Out of the dole-
fullugu-
brious copse of woodwinds
privately pranced a crazy
patchwork glockenspiel
(a very Harlequin with chin whiskers and
chamois horns)
slyly juggling
felt balls with his onyx hooves

or, succubus, tinkling
her silver tits together.

Nobody saw and laughed or gasped
or clapped his hands
or fainted dead away or nudged his neighbor.

What can you expect
in a world where the retina
receives the image upside down?

By the way,
do you know what that *WHOOM* this morning was?
No, I shouldn't put it down
to poltergeists
nor even to termites.

Maybe someday
when I am surer of it myself
I'll tell you

if you are still interested.

DIALOGUE WITH THE SPHINX

So I spoke in a chorus of three different voices:
    of a gun-shy banshee,
    of a landlocked merman,
        of Orpheus himself with a bad case
                of laryngitis,
and said, Where is this performance getting us?

And the Sphinx—at least I took her for the Sphinx:
according to the sextant,
the fix seemed right for the road to Thebes,
and she had the same firm
hoyden impersonal breasts that Ingres
                endows her with—
said, "Not much of anywhere as far as I can tell.
Where are you *trying* to get to?"
        Nowhere that I know of.
"Then you are heading the wrong way,
        turning your back on it. This is the road
from nowhere that you know of
        to nowhere that you *don't* know of."
Is there much difference?
        "How should I know? All that *I've* been to
is the nowhere that *I* know of."

So I scuffed it all out
                and started over again.

    And that was that: I had spoken with the Sphinx.

VARIATIONS ON A THRENE
FOR TRISTAN TZARA (1896–1963)

Tzara, gentil compagnon, *sage*
erstwhile infant Pope of Unreason,
in those days you decreed, "To make a poem, take
one newspaper, one pair of scissors,
snip the words one by one and put them in a bag.
Shake gently, draw them out at random,
and copy them conscientiously . . .
DADA est mort. DADA est idiot. Vive DADA!"

Let's put them in a hat—a top hat,
a fedora, fez, sombrero, a mitre if you like.
Put them *all* in, ripe ones, green ones,
the ace of spades and a tray of diamonds,
giblets of the ram that Yahweh sent in Isaac's stead,
both ears and tail—Olé!—of Pasiphaë's bull.
Baste well with centaur's seed
and garnish with sprigs of fly agaric.
One batch makes enough for ten or a dozen servings,
depending on how hungry people are—
or spread on canapés and use for appetizers.
Some of your guests will blink and go stark mad.
Others will merely become more erotic and congenial.

Say there are eleven of them. Half are now
trussed in strait jackets, receiving shock treatment,
undergoing lobotomy. The others are
a poet, a taxi driver, his twin a
taxidermist, an admiral-of-the-fleet,
and two young virginal receptionists,

one of whom will sit beside you on the sofa,
puckering her lips and drawing what looks like
an upside down map of Florida,
explaining, "Zees ees a pootzie-ket."
(She was born and raised in Akron, Ohio.) The other
will lay her hand on the admiral's lap and ask,
"What do you *really* do when you're at sea?"
The taxi driver will be playing *morra* with the poet.
The taxidermist will be urging on the lady analyst
the advantages of mounting over cremation.

> *Tzara, even when your hair was white*
> *and you were editing Rimbaud, Corbière,*
> *propounding new interpretations of Villon,*
> *based on analyses of reams of graphs,*
> *and making do with lumpier girls*
> *than a man would by choice,*
> *I saw you still*
> *as the cherub-faced Puck with the precocious monocle,*
> *launching Dada, bubbling even then*
> *with cockeyed but genuine erudition.*

Put everything—a bit of everything,
the Holy Grail, a comet's tail, Gerard
de Nerval's pet lobster
on its blue ribbon leash—in a copper vat
or cauldron, season with a pinch of Lot's wife,
and keep it at a simmer
until the Parousia or at least until
the last disgruntled waiter starts
stacking up the chains and flicking out
the lights.

> *Tzara, I don't like your being dead.*
> *Somehow you seem less cut out for it*
> *than almost any one I ever knew.*

ODE (AFTER THÉOPHILE DE VIAU, CIRCA 1620)

Somewhere before me a Crow caws,
A Shade works Horror to my Eyes,
Two Weasels and two Foxes cross
The Pathway where my going lies.
My Horse has stumbled in the Gloom.
A frothing-fit strikes down my Groom,
And Thunder cracks on every side.
Charon is calling me by name.
I see Earth's Center yawning wide.

The Brook flows back to whence it came.
Up Gothic Steeple scales an Ox,
And Blood is oozing from those Rocks.
Atop that ancient Donjon's Crest,
A Serpent rends a Vulture's Breast.
Flames within an Ice-Block race.
The Sun is blackened over all
I see the Moon about to fall.

That Tree has budged and quit its Place.

CENA AND PAROUSIA

Cat's-cradle country where the dead poets live
Their chronicles as loose as airborne thread
Spiders balloon on, this my ghost I give
To be a hostage in my poems' stead.

Corrosive canticles crack dawns apart
That were my chrysalis, fragment of the chalice
That brimmed with the pure ichor of my heart,
And angel agents of their master's malice
Harass me and my kind.
                              They smash the lyres
We thought well hidden under trundle beds:
Be phoenixes and they'll piss out your pyres;
Be vestals, they will ream your maidenheads.

Yet flaunting their disfavor, we will glut
Our thirst on tears we will not, can not, shed
And grin at being picked to be the butt
Of this capricious Barmecidal spread.

Cat's-cradle country where the heritages
Hang on gods' saying, though they never speak,
Contract your fringe of wincing oyster edges
To see us give your gods' long ears a tweak.

Cena and Parousia, the Manna
That never fell except on sabbath days
We reap and carry, wrapped in a bandana,
Along our exile road, pursued by brays.

MOMENTO

"I too have known
The terrible Gehenna of the
bone."

—EDITH SITWELL

The ultimate shade is lilies
as the mime's last grime is grey.
Jays whet their beaks on the willow's
bare branches in the rain.

    Stately shy as a shadow
    over a moorland pool
    that forgotten legends hallow,
    she mocks the fragile moon.

    Quicksilver trickles on velvet,
    albino peacocks strut—
    but a harpstring plucked by a marmoset
    wakes sap in the secret bud.

    Did ever a penknife whittle a flame?
    The lips that have nibbled the quince
    shape an anguished pantomime,
    and the shade is Hyacinth.

The blackbird sways on the cat-tail,
the swift clings tight to the wall,
and the pallid sedges rattle
like quills across the swail.

AGATHA TITTLETON

". . . a baby owl that had
fallen out of its nest, and
which used to sleep with its
head on my shoulder, pretend-
ing to snore in order to attract
mice."

—EDITH SITWELL

Trailed by the whimpering whippets of Thunder,
Where were you riding to, taller than trees,
Sipping at times from your flagon of Wonder
And drunk with the heady strong strumming of bees?

Why were you hiding those willow-smooth thighs of yours,
Firmer than candlesticks, stronger than branches?
Why were you dimming the glint of those eyes of yours,
Backs of your knuckles pressed hard to your haunches?

What were you finding and what were you losing,
Haughtily, naughtily sorting out creeds?
What were you spurning and what were you choosing,
Bartering nuggets away for glass beads?

Wildly the tom-toms were booming and throbbing,
Clashing and bashing the spangles of brass,
Sweat-soaked, the dancers were panting and sobbing.
Our little Miss Tittleton slept on the grass.

Dreams clanging like cymbals or shrill as a fife,
With jungles and deserts and coves of mauve sand,
What needs she of thimbles, what need to be wife?
Black panthers, bright lizards eat out of her hand.

Tall elm tops above her, a peacock to love her . . .
A faun in the offing to spred her asunder
Takes fright at the sight when those butterflies hover.
She wakes to surprise at the vision that stunned her.

But what shall she make of it, idyll unending,
Emerald Eden, devoid of its snake?
How much shall she take of it, sweet poison blending
Psyche's strait couch and Ophelia's lake?

A GRAVE IN APRIL

She will peep out on Judgment Day,
Shyly, till all the judging's done—
Then shed cocoon of dimity
And saunter out into the sun.

In Eve's first nakedness complete,
Seeing the dancing shadows dapple
Her belly, breasts and thighs and feet,
Serenely she will munch the apple.

Then, all the sky to be her mirror,
Suzanna, well aware the hills
are Elders, preens, makes sure they hear her
Giggle, "Let them stare their fills."

COLLOQUE D'OUTRE-TOMBE

On reading *The Marriage of Heaven and Hell,*
Not quite in a dudgeon but near it,
Emerson said, "It is very well,
But cannot the Spirit parse and spell?"

Whereat Blake rose up or Blake rose down—
Which, Billy himself could not quite tell—
Till his shadow darkened Concord town.
"And if," he howled in a Blakean blast,
"The Spirit could spell and parse,
I'm here to tell, you can bet your arse
That *you'd* be the last to hear it!"

VI

"FROM GOING TO AND FRO IN THE EARTH..."

THE MAGI

The three wise men looked equivocally
at three different stars.

The one who was fluent in Aramaic asked the shepherds,
"Are there in these place one inn?"

Impious shipwreck.
We had come well supplied
with slippers and sleeping pills
laxatives lighter fluid flea powder
inflatable mattresses and in case of need
a month's supply of prophylactics

Each saying, "I saw this star and
dropping everything, set out,
sur l'éperon du moment, comme disent les Anglais,
quite unprepared, just as I was."

We found three different Kristkinder
in three different mangers
and went home satisfied
leaving three different infants to make what they might
of frankincense and myrrh.

We have written three different books
all unpublished
each in his own tongue
telling of the hardships and perils of the voyage.

STREET SCENE: ON THEMES
BY EDVARD MUNCH

(The setting is on the Boulevard de Clichy near the gate of
the Cemetery of Montmartre.)

I

Don't scream.
It is only a thickset man in a dented derby
and black shoes run over at the heels. He walks
like a toy bear, its clockwork running down.
The scuffed black artificial leather briefcase
he is carrying under his arm because the rivet
that held the handle is torn loose contains
nothing but a last year's newspaper
and a package of expired foreclosal notices.

> By a blind malice, under the causeway
> of the rue Joseph de Maistre,
> is Stendhal's tomb, where a lady has just laid
> a bouquet of sea-lavender.

The girl in the faded pink brassière and panties
sitting at the fifth story window drying her hair
and believing herself invisible
is a waitress at the Dupont around the corner.
(One advantage of amnesia is the omniscience it confers.)
It is her day off—*repos hebdomadaire.*

Don't scream. So you do see a shoddy old archangel
with varicose veins, his atrophied, paralytic wings
concealed beneath the cape of a shabby ulster.

That is nothing to scream about. Don't look at your watch.
It is only the same time
that it was at this time yesterday.
Isn't that enough for you? . . . That is only a schnauzer
preparing to . . . Don't. Can't you see that I . . .
 I beg your pardon, was that *you* who screamed?

II

No? I see . . . I see what you were thinking of . . .
This is a street scene, in a plain explicit street.
It is approximately 10:30 of a Tuesday morning,
month and year immaterial. This is the Boulevard de Clichy,
right here in Paris. It is not
the Karl-Johans-gade in Christiania.

. . . the epitaph reads: "Visse, Scrisse, Amò."
But maybe he was only boasting—except
for the writing part. Although most people *have*
scribbled something, not everyone has lived,
not everyone has loved. We have only
his own word for it. In any case, screaming won't . . .
In a dented derby. A schnauzer or a griffon
dubiously prospecting a last year's lamppost.
That is a waitress on her day off combing
ihr goldenes Alsatian Haar. What else
is a girl to do on her day off? Don't look at your watch.
A watched watch, sage Heraclitus says, never boils.
It is a weekday mid-morning on a busy thoroughfare.
There is traffic, autobuses, camions, taxis,
thundering in all directions.
                                        The silence?
Yes, I hear it as clearly as you do,
drowning out all sound, crystalizing, crackling off
each instant into its own opaque eternity.
I hear it, but I do not think it indicates
that Judgment Day has come and passed unnoticed.

The end of the world usually makes
much more of a racket than that.
                                        Look,
let's pretend that up the street under the
plane trees a squad of lead
soldiers is practicing the manual of arms. Don't . . .
Oh, all right. Go ahead. No need to fight it.
Scream as loudly as you like. I'll join you.
Both of us. Altogether now—One, Two . . .

Pardon me, do you still want to? Neither do I.

I do not think that we have met before.
No need, I think, to say our name.
Let's go and buy a sprig or two of heather
and lay it on the tomb of Henri Beyle.

POSTSCRIPT TO A TRAVELOGUE

Shortly after the takeoff from the dirt
runway of Las Vicunhas, the LORAN went out.
Since then, flying on compass course all day,
our azimuth has borne over a level upland
spreading to all horizons, uninhabited,
unmarked by road or valley.
Late afternoon we make a bumpy landing
on a plain splotched with clumps of pampas grass.
You are the only passenger. A one-eyed official,
unshaven, wearing a faded uniform
with a torn collar and missing several buttons,
approaches. Wiping sleep from his single eye,
he takes a pistol from a box-like holster,
breaks it, blows the dust out of the barrel,
and puts a bullet through the pilot's brain.
He inspects the plane, walking slowly around it,
with a whistle, summons a lame underling even shabbier
than himself and gives an order in what sounds
like Aymarán or Quechuan. While the underling
is sloshing down the plane with gasoline
and touching a match to it, singeing himself
badly as he does, the official demands your passport,
pockets it and tells you you are refused
permission to land. He climbs into a jeep
and throws it into gear. The underling
gives a dog-like moan and flounders after it.
Just as he seems about to catch it,
the official jams it into quick reverse.
The underling plops like a crushed cockroach.

The jeep takes off across the plain,
backfiring as it goes.

On the unhinged door of the tarpaper shack
a scrawled notice reads: NO TRESPASSING.
THIS AIRPORT IS PERMANENTLY CLOSED.

All about cicadas zizz. Puff adders
rustle among the dry stalks of grass,
refuse to let themselves be tamed.
There is a rusted can of Spam upon the shelf
behind the dispatcher's counter
and a broken clasp knife you can use to open it.
The ants appear. It is like a tarvia skin
rippling of its own volition. On the fifth day
bald-necked buzzards circle and flop down
to strip the underling's and pilot's bones.

On the eleventh day an ancient gray wolf spider
plods its way across the threshold and topples dead.
Its hair droops over its eyes like a Skye terrier's.

From that day on there is no movement. Ants and adders
have disappeared. The air never stirs.
The cicadas have long been silent.

On the day that would have been the autumn solstice
except, as you now notice, that the sun,
since that first afternoon you landed,
has hung motionless on a flat
uncurving sky—
                    you find a pencil stub
in a pocket of the pilot's jacket
and are about to scratch a message
in the caked dust-coating of the windowpane,
only to discover
your mind can no more shape your name.

94

WUNDAY THE WORST OF WEPTOBER

I

As of Wunday the Worst of Weptober,
it was open season on everything:
on Sun and Moon, on Traffic Lights
and all eight Planets,
Whirlpools and Whippoorwills,
Doppelgangers and Divinities.

A Woodchuck could sit on the edge of its hole
and take pot shots—bang! bang!—at
State Troopers whizzing by on motorcycles . . .

Open season on everything but Seasons.

II

Gravely, as in a ritual rehearsed
till all its once significance is lost,
Shrewd Blunders walked the empty streets, conversed
of meaning in the Holy Holocaust.

And in confessional Father Gillhooly
plied Mrs. Potiphar with queries till
she muttered mousetalk, never answered truly,
nor is it likely that she ever will.

Unruly echoes roll beneath the sky
the rusty rut of behemoth and ape.

Flesh answers *how* while Mind still stammers, "Why?"
Lust kneads the marrow to the needed shape.

III

Says Caliban grown old, "I feel no grief
but that the end of time has come and gone,
left unfulfilled its promise to be brief.

——Tails, I'm a lemur: heads, a leprechaun.

"Heads, I'm the head wherein the dream I stalk
scurries in vain and soon must go to earth.
Tails, I'm the dream itself and in it walk
a dizzy tight-rope strung from death to birth.

"Heads, I'm a wizard conjuring a spell
at will so artfully that even I,
lolling in this snug palace where I dwell,
need never notice that it is a sty.

"Or, tails, I am a puppet; yet the strings
that twitch my arms and legs and bend my spine
in minuets or jigs or Highland flings
are part of me—my nerves and therefore mine.

"All but invisible these strands!
Yet clear enough to the observant
they will be seen to lead to hands
and hence to brain, in turn their servant.

> "*Tails? Say, that I should give the tail a twist?*
> *Seeing the ante, choose to up it?*
> *Could I extinguish the ventriloquist*
> *by switching off the puppet?*"

The Seven Sleepers speak their dream
that sifts through words as through a sieve.
Vestals in tattered panties scream
aloud their muffled wish to live.

The Seven Sleepers live their dream
mulled through the ten score years gone by.
Sad demons shake their heads and deem
they should have seized their chance to die.

In Ephesus the Sleepers wake
to thundering shafts and howling gears
and bleat, "Oh, for sweet Jesus' sake!"
stuffing their fingers in their ears.

But what of us who *never* sleep
but only watch the hours creep
through alleyways of Ephesus
from dawn to dawn? Oh, what of us?

We preen our braggadocio
as spell against the floorboards' creak
of night by dark, who by day so
deplore the mumblings of the weak.

We envy Winok'h in his cell
calling for blood—aye, blood for Christ!
Chains flailing walls. The clamors swell
for blood we find too highly priced.

(The truth is one cannot confide
to wife or friendly whore or friend,
"There is a nightmare I must ride
to where its aberrations end.")

V

On Wunday the Worst of Weptober,
the dreamers and schemers alike,
shouted, "Come, we have been too long sober,
and life is a punch we must spike."

On Shrewsday the Fast of Dead-ember,
the Ephesus Sleepers awoke
and laughingly chanced to remember
that their whole lifelong dream was a joke.

On Mensday and Cursday and Sighday
of the deadest and dreadest of weeks,
aging Caliban mumbles, "When's *my* day?"
He grumbles and bumbles, "When's *my* day?
I don't ask for a pie-in-the-sky day.
All I want is a lie-down-and-die day."
But the gods stop their ears when he speaks.

VI

> Caliban: *Oh ho!—would it had
> been done!
> Thou didst prevent me; I
> had peopled else
> This isle with Calibans.*
>   —The Tempest

Unmoved by solar orbits sprung awry,
The Princess in the meadow croons a threne
For all the feckless ghosts that cannot die,
For all the lilies shriveled in their sheen,

For every nuptial bed whose shredded sheet
Is knotted into noose, for toppled chair,
For marble floor just skimmed by dangling feet,
For nipples left unkissed, unmingled hair,

98

Even for Caliban's unpeopled isle
Still taunted by the fragrance of Miranda.
Father Gilhooly, plump parthenophile,
Peeps through the alders, praying in the while
Saint Nicholas will send her comfort and a
Great cuddly plush, yet somehow sentient, panda.

VII

Enter Ariel in the air
ringing hands as if a bell,
bloody sockets, skull laid bare,
onetime song a gasping yell:

"Love quickly, lovers,
scramble into bed!
Oh, look not up to where the dun cloud hovers!
Quickly let those thighs be spread
while their spell still holds its power!
Quickly!
With the aimless dead
you may lie within the hour.

"Quickly, plowman, till the field
if only for a crop of tares.
You will never reap its yield;
give it still your last of cares.

"Hurry, potter, twirl your wheel,
willing a last shape to clay
in this hour when the steel-
shod centaurs stamp and champ and neigh.

"Singer, make us a last song,
of simple words for men to die by,
words to read—if not for long—
our fading shadow on the sky by."

VIII

Tongue swells in the mouth, the hand falters.
Our roots have gone dead in the ground.
Infant corpses lie quartered on altars.
The hero moans, deep in his mound.
The arches and obelisks crumble,
and oak trunks in agony twist.
The plain does its best to dissemble
an incontrovertible list.

On that Wunday the Worst of Weptober
when werewolves revert into men
and the blood-drunken Winok'hs fall sober,
who'll invent gods to pardon us then—
coin Molochs to pardon us then?

MONGOOSE

It is not merely
that the mongoose is quicker than the cobra,
its tactics less predictable,
its counter-clockwise feints so swift
that the reptile's lunges lapse
into slow motion
nor that, putting its own
fluffed fur to fine advantage,
it is not at all impressed
by the cobra's puffed-out hood
and reads correctly
the flickering tongue as only
a measure of bewilderment.

It is not merely
that he holds the initiative
in what for him is play
that practice has made him
uncannily proficient at . . .

    His chief advantage is that
he can break the skirmish off at will,
resume whenever the fancy takes him,
always on his own terms.

    Strike or not strike,
the odds remain the same.
He can no more be parried than propitiated . . .

though comfort may perhaps be found
in believing that he does not exist
    or is benevolent . . .
or even in the thought that,
given the initial capital and finding takers,

    we cobras could make fortunes
    by wagering against ourselves.

AUTOPHAGE

Even when doing nothing, I am still
doing all that *can* be done, working like—
    what has a beaver masticating aspens
or a Trojan munching wooden horsemeat
got on me?
In just this moment, beginning with the
condyle of the humerus, I've gnawed
my way up to the extensor communis digitorum,
by nightfall shall have reached
the deltoid's lower ligaments.
Tomorrow in between answering want-ads—
everything from Executive Engineering Director
at a starting salary of $40,000, to
"salesman for household novelty appliances,
no experience required"—and ghosting
autobiographies, I shall take a break
to devour my left sternocleidomastoid.
By Michaelmas, all that remains of me will be
the upper outside quadrant of the right
gluteus maximus, which I am saving
for a final snack on Twelfth-Night.

What I shall find then to keep me occupied
when not breeding guppies, winding my watch,
or supervising digging graves for friends
on days the sexton is too drunk to hold a plumb-line,
I can't imagine. It worries me.
Sometimes I would get down on my
(if I had not improvidently eaten them)
rotulae
and pray.

VII

SALUTE TO
SUNDRY

TO A FACE IN THE MÉTRO

Lad, you with the flabby briefcase
between you miming a pietà by Murillo
or, so help us, Greuze,
listen:
No one could ever be as woe-begone
as you are straining to look. No,
even if both your parents had died in their infancy
and the only girl you ever loved had run away
with an albino Eskimo while you were yet in diapers,
there would be no excuse for the pained vacuity
of those brown-cow eyes, that crinkled brow,
and mouth like a lugubrious circumflex
lamenting a lost chin.

Of *course*, the world is evil!
Although you have not lived long enough to know it,
scoundrels' whims defined the destinies
of all of us before you were *in ovo*,
and evidences of a benevolent God
range at best from negative to slim.
But such, I trust, are not the stems of your distress.

What *are* you, lad? twenty-two or three? and still
wondering where your first piece is coming from?
I'll tell you:
As long as you go on wearing that look
of the early bird that swallowed the wrong worm,
it's not coming from anywhere.

Look, try this:
zip up that briefcase. Hoist those doleful dewlaps.
Grin—or if you can't grin,
at least try to imagine yourself grinning
(I can't help you there: I can't imagine that mouth
doing anything but spitting prune pits).
Resolve that you will spend an hour a day
not trying to feel so sorry for yourself.
Come on, lad: put your hair on straight,
quit mooning at your eyebrows and balancing
hypothetical angels on your nose.
Breathe as if you didn't live in dread
of dislocating your diaphragm . . .
And before you know, some flicker-tailed nixette
will pounce
and shake you into life and make you *like* it.

Right now
you are mulishly convinced
that you could never deign to like *anything*.
But try it, lad. Deigning is simple.
Just follow these well-meant directions. Then
if they don't work out, it still won't be
too late to take that jump into the Seine.
No one will mind it, either. You can even take
that briefcase with you. There are
too many people and *far* too many
briefcases
in the world anyway.

HOMAGE TO GOLO GRUMPELT

Look, first let's get this straight:
you know *me;* I'm not trying to take
anything away from the New Realism crowd,
Rauschenberg or Jasper Johns' flags with exactly the right
number of stars and stripes on them—that guy can *count!*—
nor Oldenburg's plaster ice-cream cones and hamburgers
so real they make you want to up-chuck,
nor Tinguely's stuff that blows itself to pieces
when you push a button, nor this Hungarian
that makes constructions that fall apart faster
than he can put them together, so that when he's finished,
he isn't even back to where he started from.
He's *got* something! They've *all* got something.
I've got to hand it to them, sure.

                                  It's just that *you*
have got it over all of them. You *have*
what they only think they've got. Take for instance
that time at the West Side Independents' show:
this jerk that comes in with a plastic toilet seat
with bent nails, points out, glued all over it.
You get the symbolism? It's corny, what?
so corny it makes you want to cry. The point is
then *you* come in with just that cardboard box
you got a taxi to run over and then
wrapped a piece of baling wire around it.
That was pure! What the French call *absolu,* if you know
what I mean. And when the guy that runs the gallery
wants to hang it on the wall like it was meant
to be a masterpiece or something,

you kick it into a corner and tell him,
"Leave it there, see!" And the guy does see
and before the show is over, he sells it for five hundred—
well, all right, fifty—dollars. Anyway,
the principle's the same.

Sometimes I just can't help comparing *you*
with—well, mentioning no names, because
some of them are friends of both of us—
but like that Guggenheim show where the guy
enters a pair of blue jeans dipped in plaster
with sardine cans riveted to the knees.
You can't *object* to stuff like that except that it shows
how far some guys will go to be original.
Like Fred entering that plain eight-foot-by-six
canvas with a lipstick on a chain
nailed to the stretcher for people to write or draw
on it. Anything to be original! Now, *you*
wouldn't be found dead *trying* to be original.
Being original, yes, but trying to be, no.
Like the time you stuck a special delivery stamp
on a paper bag filled with Coca Cola caps
and nailed it up in an orange crate and nailed *that*
to the floor so that the only way the public
could see into it was by lying on their bellies
and peeking through a crack—
and entitled it *Déjà Vu!*
Man! if anybody else had done that, it would have stunk.
Know why? Because it would have been obvious.
That's why. But when *you* do it,
obvious is the very thing it isn't.
That's why, when some schnook asks me who is the most
significant artist in the world today,
I look him in the eye and say, "Who're you kidding?
Ever hear of a guy named Golo Grumpelt?"

HOMAGE TO CYRUS FLORAC ON THE OCCASION OF THE PREMIERE AT THE SALLE PLEYEL OF HIS CONCERTO IN 3 HOURS ♭

At exactly, so the tickets warned, 8:30,
vue the solemnity of the occasion, the doors
would be rigorously closed and all access
to the auditorium thereafter be denied.

        So, precisely
at 9 hours twenty, a skaggle of assorted
long-necked, pinch-beaked countesses and duchesses
straight out of the Almanach de Gotha
began to start to trickle in,
flashing lorgnettes, unfurling stoles and boas
with little ostrich squawks as if being diffidently goosed
by a retinue of shy
ancestral cold-nosed lycanthropes.

Next, at the very nick of 9:47,
this conductor who always looked as if—
well, skip it. Wumpelschnecht,
let's say the name was. And, if you've ever seen
him on a podium, you will recall
what contretemps he always looked as if
had just happened to him—momentarily emerged.

        Whereat hopefully
oboe lowed the pitch and, to the scuffle of
adjusting stands and distributing parts, tentatively
fiddles twiddled, bassoons oomed and kettledrum
gave forth experimental bongs . . .
                       and,

having for the moment keyed our hopes,
subsided.

Then suddenly, on the approximately very dot
of 10:15, in ambled like an avuncular
old borborygmic tarantula-in-residence,
none other than the Master in person,
which, as it turned out,
was what we had been waiting for all along.

There was an ecstatic little pitter-patter of dessicated
ladyfingers, and all the countesses and duchesses,
together with a slew of odd princesses or two,
twilled and twuttered,
got their harnds keessed languidly by heem
and he gart hees harnds keessed in turn by them
and copiously called more *cher Maîtres* and *très cher Maîtres*
than you could brandish a bâton at.

Which brings us up to 11:17.

As for the concerto itself—
once the musicians were finally rounded up again
and the rare people who had *paid* for their tickets
but had to catch the last Métro, had left—
since it *was* a première, everybody
        (except me) agreed
that it was very nice.

GEORGE TROCKETT

I

I'd like to find him words as lumbering and unlicked
as his own outsized frame and bulk it carried.
The lawyers and surveyors, actuaries
called his cubicle "the bear pit" and professed
to pity us "boy sleuths" who worked for him.

Put him roughly at six feet four or five,
two-hundred-fifty-odd tobacco-chewing pounds,
George Trockett in suspenders, brass collar button
and no collar, small blue ursine eyes asquint
through gummy steel-rimmed glasses—puckered jowls,
glum creases at the corners of his mouth.
Something between an Ajax drawn by Baskin
and Titan in a Goya lithograph,
the whole as out of place in a Wall Street office
of the Associated Shipowners' Mutual Indemnity
as Falstaff at a tea on Beacon Hill.

II

With no help ever from the man himself,
I gleaned and pieced together, following somewhat
Trockett's own method, unraveling link by link,
a fragment of his legend. It begins—
before that everything is blank—with his leaving
Harvard Law School in his last term to take
a job as Chief of Police

at the St. Louis Fair. That sets the date
at 1904 or so. Hiatus then
of half a dozen years. Spent how and where?
My random guess favored San Francisco.
Trying a lead one day, I mentioned cable-cars:
he gave me a slow glare and sent me out
to check a 'tween-decks plan at Erie Basin.
Central or South America perhaps:
once I thought I sensed him following the Spanish
passed between a Puerto Rican runner and his client.
Somewhere along the way he'd come to know
freighters, from plates to crow's nests.

III

He came to Wall Street via one of those
periodicals that thrive on items like:
"We learn with pleasure that T. Whitcomb Whoozis,
last year acquitted by a hung jury of embezzlement
and subornation in Chicago, has become
a partner in the investment brokerage firm
of Sisyphus & Beelzebub."
Before it went to press, the galley proofs
were sent to Mr. Whoozis with request
to check inaccuracies and make
suggestions or deletions—please no checks—
bills preferred in small denominations.

George Trockett's job was digging up the facts
and steering course just short of actionable slander,
an art that so appealed to a perverse
wry whimsy in him he might well have spent
his life at it if, at Christmastime,
the idea had not come to his employers
to give the man a bonus. Trockett refused.
It wasn't, he explained, that he despised

money more than the next man, but that his fancy
didn't run to taking bribes from blackmailers.

The story got about, though not through Trockett.
A former law-schoolmate, Chairman by then
of the Shipowners' Mutual, remembering him
as a diamond in the rough, took him on to head
the Accident Department. Some days later,
with the thought perhaps to rehabilitate him,
restore the fellow's self-respect, made the mistake
of asking him to dinner. Trockett stumped
into the front office, sputtering with rage.
He'd work, he said, for anyone that paid him,
but *where,* with *whom* and *what* he ate
were his own concern. And, while he was about it,
he'd had enough of crawling on his knees
to get some sniveling typist from the pool.
He wanted that Jew girl—the dog-faced one—name of Goldfarb—
to be his secretary. Was that clear?

IV

He gave good measure, used his looming bulk
and bull of Bashan bellow to browbeat
claimants and witnesses. He doctored evidence,
induced runners to sell out on their clients,
counted as lost the day he neither made a new
or confirmed an old, enmity. Wily, tough,
as full of twists as a donkey-engine's cable,
mean as a drunk longshoreman's cargo hook,
Trockett, who claimed his only use for books
was as doorstops or paperweights, soon knew
as many tricky points of maritime law
as anybody on our legal staff.
His brief, *Zatrapalik vs. S/S Silverlake,*
established that a seaman's catching mumps
on a chartered ship of Panamanian registry

is "an act of God" within the meaning of the term.
"Remember," he admonished me, "that God
and the King's enemies are the claims agent's best friends."

V

[*Trockett
receives.*]

Thumbs hooked in his suspenders, back propped
against the door, "Look here, buster," (Buster being
the Honorable Gideon Z. Goodell, co-author of
the Seamen's Compensation Act) "this client of yours . . .
The first time that he got his ear lobe chewed
by a rat was on the S/S *Ocean Eagle,*
sailing from Bordeaux. We settled for
two hundred dollars, of which you gave him maybe twenty.
That's no affair of mine: even ambulance chasers—
though God knows why—have got a right to live.
His name was Julio Gonzales—right?
The next time that it happened was six months later.
S/S *Epirus* carrying kips and figs
out of Smyrna. By now the name's Zatrides.
I gave you fifty bucks then on a package deal.
Now he turns up named Galazzo and the rat
bit him on the *Blue Fox* out of Monrovia.
This time we've got it all sewed up though.
A rat? Look, we've matched the toothmarks. They belong
to a hooker in Weehawken named Conchita.
Sure, I can put her on the witness stand
and offer her denture as Exhibit A.
I'm settling for five dollars just to show
there's no hard feelings. What's next on your list?
Fella named Jonah, deck passenger to Tarshish,
charging ship's negligence for letting him
get swallowed by a whale?"

116

His enemy was THEY—THEY, the nameless
people who owned or wished they owned
estates on Long Island, houses in Westchester,
apartments on Park Avenue, THEY who made the laws,
THEY who *belonged,* who went to opening nights,
periodically had friends in to dinner
and perhaps played bridge or poker afterward,
the sorry slobs and slobbesses who either
thought that they were happy or *wished* to think
that they were happy and who, worst of all,
wanted to make other people, far and near,
be happy too, THEY who would never quit
until they'd found
a shirt-tail for every little bare backside
in Senegambia,
THEY, who in summertime packed off the shrill,
unwashed, unkillable, stickball playing
infants of the slums to hygienic rural
areas where they lost both their precariously
acquired immunities and their inborn
dexterity at dodging trucks.

THEY, he was convinced, were everywhere—
tailing him in streets, hidden behind the files,
listening in ventilator shafts. Why not?
"Every time I pass a sewer grill,
I'm almost afraid to look for fear I'll see
one of those pinstriped rats peeking out of it.
Hm. The way I rant, you'd think I had
a persecution complex—as I well may have.
A man's got to have *something* to while away the time.
I haven't any wives or kids, I don't collect
stamps or first editions or write poetry
or watch any birds, except sometimes pigeons."

VII

That afternoon he had put on
tantrums that rated well among his best.
When he had ramped and raged his fill and driven
the filing clerk to tears, with fist upraised
like Moses coming down from Horeb, cowed
the trig Bostonian office manager, torn
a trial lawyer's finished brief to shreds—
he slammed the door.

                A grin of slightly fiendish
innocence lit his face. He leaned above my desk,
great puppy paw plopped on the report
that I was trying to write, and jerked his head
toward the outer office. "Listen, you know what?
They think I'm crazy, and the joke's on them:
they're right and they don't know it. Only you
and Goldie know it, and even I'm not sure
you really believe it.
I'd quit this job tomorrow if I was right in the head,
and marry Goldie and take up chicken farming
somewhere in Connecticut or Jersey."

    "Trockett," Goldie said, "if the last man on this earth
had just been put to beddy-bye in Woodlawn cemetery
and you were God Himself with a million dollars
right in your hip pocket, I wouldn't think
of marrying you."

                "What about *two* million, Goldie?"
"Two million? Now *there* I'd have to stop and think.
Make it an even three, I'd be a pushover."

    "Would you now, Goldfarb? Look, I'll tell you what:
if they had only put that brain of yours behind
a face that looked less like a traffic cop's,
I'd almost wish I *had* three million dollars."

    "Aw, quit that pretty-talking me, Georgie boy.
You make me feel so good I want to cry."

    "*That* would be the day, Goldie."

    "It would, at that. The last time I cried was when

the midwife held me up and smacked my fanny.
The next time I cry will be at my own funeral."
    "You will? What for? What's wrong with being dead?"
    "Nothing that I know of except the way
those undertakers gyp you. But at a funeral,
somebody's got to cry, and if I don't,
who will?"
                    "Why, I would, Goldie. Just you let me know
when it is going to be and where. I'll send
a singing telegram that says, 'boo-hoo!'"
    "I bet you would, Trockett, old heart of gold.
I'd appreciate it. And I'll send you back
a telegram that says, real lady-like,
'S for Sammy, H for Hyman, I
for Irving—and a great big T for you,
Trockett'—meaning no disrespect."

One morning Goldie packed him home with flu.
"Not brains enough to know when you are sick?
Or want to give it to the rest of us?"
She sent an office boy to get a taxi.
Sorting his mail, she said, "You know,
sometimes that big baboon is almost human."
    "Just how?" I asked.
                    "Oh, I don't know. It's hard
to put a finger on it. Just sort of human.
That's more than you can say for most folks."

    The day I told him I was leaving, going back
to France for no clear reason except I wanted to,
he chomped his cud a while. "Well, that makes sense.
A man just can't go wrong doing what he wants to.
I tried it once but didn't follow through.
You won't either. Nobody ever does. It's worth
the try though."
                    As I was clearing out my desk,
he said, "If you're not eating somewhere else tonight,

I know a Greek place where the food's no worse
than in most other joints. Go dutch, I mean . . .
No, come to think of it, it's closed on Friday.
Maybe when you come back—about next year."

VIII

"IT IS MEET THAT GREEKS SHOULD RULE OVER BARBARIANS"

—ARISTOTLE

HOMAGE TO
JOHN FOSTER DULLES

(For his Effort to set up a Dictatorship for his Friend Ngo Dinh Diem. 1961.)

I always say that when an American is traveling abroad
he or she should try to be a sort
of unofficial good-will ambassador, if you know what I mean.
Not necessarily chauvinistic, but brightening up
our national image, so to speak.
So whenever in my travels I hear anybody repeating
that slogan, "The only good Yankee is a dead Yankee"—
as one increasingly does since American advisors
moved into Vietnam and began advising genocide
as an antidote for anticolonialism
and illustrating their point by basting babies in napalm,
tying naked boys by the wrists to tanks
and dragging them through brooks, and other
equally whimsical G.I. pranks—
    Yessir! Every time I hear this line
about dead Americans being good ones,
I speak right up and say, "Oh, yeah?
Well, what about John Foster Dulles?
He's dead, isn't he?"

THE RESEDA AND THE ROSE

(*From the French of Louis Aragon*)

(Aragon dedicates this poem, written and widely circulated clandestinely during the Nazi occupation of France, to four heroes—or, as the Germans called them, "terrorists"—of the Résistance, two of them Catholics, the others Communists. The original text, which I have tried to follow faithfully in all other respects, uses only two rhyme-sounds.)

He who believed in heaven
He who did not believe
Adored the lovely captive
The booted soldiers grieve
Which of them climbed the ladder
Which of them watched below
The one who believed in heaven
The one who did not know
What does it matter
What name is given
To the light that guided their feet
Both of them died that she shall live
In the dawn that we shall greet
He who believed in heaven
And he who did not believe
One turned in at the chapel door
One of them turned aside
But both were true to a faith denied
And held to the oath they swore
That she should live who was said had died

Both of them, salt and leaven
Of hope that cannot deceive
He who believed in heaven
And he who did not believe
When the wheat is slashed by the hail
Bickerings wrong or right
Are drowned in the howl of the gale
Side by side in the fight
Stand he who believes in heaven
And he who holds to his doubt
A footstep crunched in the snow
From the wall of the citadel
A sentry's shots rang out
One of them staggered one of them fell
Which died? which crawled through the field below
Staunching his blood with his sleeve?
The one who believed in heaven
Or the one who did not believe?

Which of them in their prison
Sleeps on the softer stone?
Which cares for the rat's derision?
Which suffers the more alone
When the dank cold bites to the bone
He who believes in a heaven
Or he who believes in none?

A rebel is a rebel
At the break of the cruelest dawn
Our sobs for both are a single knell
Our grief for them both is one
For him who believed in heaven
And him who believed in none
As the eastern sky grows grey
They utter a single name
The name of the captive they both may say
Who never brought her shame
He who believed in heaven

And he who believed in none
Their life that was freely given
Their life and their death were one
And the red of their blood is the same
As it seeps in the soil they love
Though one held his faith to the earth alone
And one to heaven above

One of them—which of them—who can say?
One of them runs and one has wings
From Brittany or the Franche-Comté
When once again the cricket sings

Call it flute or call it cello
In their double love that glows
Crocus or jonquil, lark or swallow,
Dark or fair, peach or pear,
Who shall quibble Who shall care
If she who was a captive wear
At her bosom, in her hair
The reseda and the rose?

SOME OF US
MUST REMEMBER

Some of us must remember.
(Who would have thought that any could forget?)
Some of us must remember.
We owe it to our living, to our dead,
to those who tried to cross the wheatfield
                              at Château-Thierry,
the beaches of Anzio, Tarawa, Omaha,
to those who stuck the winter out
                              at Valley Forge.
We owe it to children in playpens and in wombs.
Yes, it will whet old anguishes
but some of us *must* remember.

"Wholesale arson and murder . . .
Against the terrorism and destruction from the skies
were pitted only the courage and deep faith
of the people and their priests."
No, this is not *Pravda* nor *The Manchester Guardian*
reporting on the latest antics of Westmoreland.
(Some of us must remember—*must* remember.)
This is the good-grey, right-of-center
New York Times—April, '37: the place, remember?

                              GUERNICA

Shot all males above 16, shipped all the women
to extermination camps, the children
to destinations not as yet revealed,
burned and bulldozed the village to the ground.
Do you remember? June of '42:

                              LIDICE

Rounded up the men in barns and hosed them down
with automatic rifles. Crammed the women and children
(even the newborn are potential Communists)
into the church and gutted it with phosphorus bombs:
500 by the nearest count
of calcinated skulls. One woman crawled
through a window of the apse. A boy hid in a hedge.
Looted the village house by house before
dynamiting and firing it. Remember?
The shell still stands. June 1944: the name,

ORADOUR–SUR–GLANE

How trivial such pranks seem to us now!
PHU LY   QUANG NGAI   NAM DINH   BEN TRE
We skip the names and snicker at the quip
of Madame Nhu on "barbecued Buddhists."

Ben Tre, a pleasant city, provincial capital,
some 40,000 souls, canals bordered by evergreens and mangoes,
market center for textiles, copra, palm oil, rice.
    The bombs and shells the more effective for surprise.
Among the rubble that had been homes, shawled women
squat, rocking to and fro, and moan.
Straight-faced, an Army major explained, "It became
necessary to destroy this town to save it."
In the days when soldiers still were soldiers,
he would have achieved a twisted grin of sorts
    and set his pistol to his temple,
leaving a note requesting he be spared
burial with military honors.

Some of us must remember . . . must remember.

Oh, who has stripped us of the sense of shame and horror
and robbed us of the precious gift of tears?

SCHERZO FOR A DIRGE

This boy wrote . . . I don't know him, never had
heard of him . . . class of '66, dropped out
and went to help with California migrant laborers
(sounds like a do-gooder to me, one of those
potential Terroristen that the Gestapo
loved to give the works to before they turned them over—
what was left of them—to a firing squad) . . .
wrote to me enclosing a copy of the letter he had sent
returning his draft card to the local board
"as an act of total disobedience," it states.
"In the present circumstances, I must go beyond
mere pacifist, conscientious-objector, coöperation."
Goes on to quote Thoreau: "If the law
is of such a nature that it requires you
to be an agent of injustice to another,
then, I say, break the law."
                              "Can you," the boy asks,
"help me in this cause in any way?
Friends tell me that, noble as it may be,
what I am doing is like trying
to tunnel through a mountain with a teaspoon."

Yes, it is *that* all right. Wise friends you've got.
And no, I cannot help you, can't even pray for you.
President Johnson prays. He poses for press photographs
with bowed head, thumb holding his right eyelid shut,
auricular performing the same service for the left,
his three other fingers poised against his forehead.

It takes a very pious man to pray that fervently
with flash-light bulbs exploding all around him.

I am not that pious. When I close my eyes,
my sight turns back to Guernica, Oradour, Lidice,
Ben Tre and goes sick with shame and grief.
My only prayer would be, "Listen, Lord God of Hosts,
whatever it is that you are up to, please
lay off it, for Jesus' sake. Amen."

POSTLUDE: FOR GOYA

(1938)

A bloody day subsided: the volcano's lips
cool to slag, its glow a tracery
faint against the sky. (Oh, there is still
a sky.) How different this calm from peace.
We are too shattered now to count our losses.
What is there left but loss? Who still can hope
that because we fought, others will fight,
because we were broken that earth still holds
some traces of a destiny?

We are alone tonight, each of us alone,
before and after a storm, breathing in a lull,
caught in a bight of ashy slackness.
A broad lightning painted on the sky shows livid
two skinned bulls, motionless, backed off
from goring one another. We crouch
behind a knoll of pumice and the dry clouds lie
so near above us we could reach a hand
almost to touch them. There is dust in our mouths.
Beads of useless power
exude like gum from the earth and sounds
are sucked from our lips by silence. At our feet
the bones of a buzzard lie beside
the shadowy fox's bones that stalked it.
You stare at a dry hollow and your lips
peel back from your teeth
and your shoulders mean laughter
remembering it lately was a brook.
(We must not shrink to gauge our madness,

the heat-sprung brain and fingers brittle as
scorched ivory, eyes with certain visions
baked into them.) This is not an end,
only an interlude: after a while
we will creep forth and search among the crevices
for seeds and cover them with dust
and try for tears to quicken them.
Remember only this is not an end.
We cannot win—though we perhaps have won
if we can only believe
that this is not the end.